The Eiffel Tower: The History of Paris

By Charles River Editors

Benh Lieu Song's picture of the Eiffel Tower from the Champs de Mars

About Charles River Editors

Charles River Editors provides superior editing and original writing services across the digital publishing industry, with the expertise to create digital content for publishers across a vast range of subject matter. In addition to providing original digital content for third party publishers, we also republish civilization's greatest literary works, bringing them to new generations of readers via ebooks.

Sign up here to receive updates about free books as we publish them, and visit Our Kindle Author Page to browse today's free promotions and our most recently published Kindle titles.

Introduction

Peter L. Svendsen's 2001 picture of the Eiffel Tower

The Eiffel Tower

"Being the most striking manifestation of the art of metal structures by which our engineers have shown in Europe, it is one of the most striking of our modern national genius." – Gustave Eiffel

It was the home of kings, emperors, and aristocrats. It was the home of the Champs-Élysées, the Bastille, the Louvre and the salons that fueled the Enlightenment. For foreigners like

Benjamin Franklin, it was the most beautiful city in the world, and millions of people still visit those same sites every year. Known as the "City of Light," Paris seamlessly blends its rich past with all the trappings of a modern city, and the city's features and qualities are taken for granted today, but Paris was not always that way. In fact, it took nearly half a century of redesigning the city during the 19th century to transform it into the city it is today.

Paris's expansion also required new monuments, administrative buildings, and other public buildings. The urban renewal of Paris coincided with the Neoclassicism movement in art and architecture that had taken hold across Europe, which incorporated the classical architecture of the Ancient Greeks and Romans. All over Paris, builders constructed marble colored buildings with arches, pillars, domes, and neoclassical art that used the themes of antiquity.

Fittingly, the construction of the Eiffel Tower for the 1889 World's Fair was a capstone of sorts to the reconstruction of Paris, and it remains one of the world's most famous and visited landmarks. Designed as an entrance to the fair, the Eiffel Tower, soaring over 1,050 feet into the air, was an architectural wonder that served as the world's tallest man-made object for over 40 years. As its designer, Gustave Eiffel, put it, "It seems to me that [if] it had no other rationale than to show that we are not simply the country of entertainers, but also that of engineers and builders called from across the world to build bridges, viaducts, stations and major monuments of modern industry, the Eiffel Tower deserves to be treated with consideration."

Though it may be hard to believe today, the Eiffel Tower was initially met with derision by many Frenchmen, some of whom compared it to the Tower of Babel and complained that the "useless and monstrous" structure would obscure treasures such as Notre Dame. In response to such criticisms, Eiffel himself pointed out, "Can one think that because we are engineers, beauty does not preoccupy us or that we do not try to build beautiful, as well as solid and long lasting structures? Aren't the genuine functions of strength always in keeping with unwritten conditions of harmony? ... Besides, there is an attraction, a special charm in the colossal to which ordinary theories of art do not apply."

It's safe to say that Eiffel was correct. Each year, millions of people refute those original notions by riding to the top and making it the most visited paid monument in the entire world. Indeed, the Eiffel Tower has welcomed over 250 million visitors in less than 130 years. Eiffel had the good fortune of being vindicated in his lifetime, and as he once joked, "I ought to be jealous of the tower. She is more famous than I am."

The Eiffel Tower: The History of Paris' Most Famous Landmark traces the history of the landmark from its construction to the present day. Along with pictures of important people, places, and events, you will learn about the Eiffel Tower like never before, in no time at all.

The Eiffel Tower: The History of Paris' Most Famous Landmark
About Charles River Editors
Introduction
   Chapter 1: The Great Wonder
   Chapter 2: The Employment of Iron
   Chapter 3: The Noble Structure
   Chapter 4: The First Stage of the Tower
   Chapter 5: Mathematical Considerations
   Chapter 6: Un Fait Accompli
   Chapter 7: This Stupendous Undertaking
   Online Resources
   Bibliography

Chapter 1: The Great Wonder

"The height of this great wonder of the 19th century will, when complete, be nearly 1,000 feet. … The entire structure is built of iron, the total weight of which is some 7,531 tons — say 15,062,000 pounds. Over 2,500,000 rivets will be required to put this gigantic structure together. The Tower stands some 300 yards off the south side of the Seine, near the Jena Bridge, and its base forms an immense archway over the main path leading from this bridge to the central grounds of the Exhibition. The Tower at its base covers an area of 107,584 square feet. The first floor will be devoted to cafes, restaurants, smoking room for ascenders, and as a look-out. The third floor will be the great look-out, or as some have called it, the "Alpine reception room," over which comes the cupola, which again in its turn will offer the daring ones a still higher surface from which to look down on the world nearly a 1,000 feet below. It will be something to be able to say you have been to the top of this enormous Tower." - *The Eiffel Tower, Paris, 1889*, published by F. C. Hagen & Co.

During the mid-1880s, word spread throughout France that the nation would be hosting the 1889 Exposition Universelle, better known as the World's Fair, and the theme of the Fair would be a celebration of the French Revolution. All the leading artists and inventors in the nation were encouraged to present ideas for display, and among those hoping to snag a position of honor were Maurice Koechlin and Émile Nouguier, senior engineers with the Compagnie des Établissements Eiffel, a construction company owned by Alexandre Gustave Eiffel. According to a rather fawning biographical sketch published about him at the time of the Tower's completion, "M. Gustav Eiffel is already well known as one of the ablest, boldest, and most famous French engineers, and was born in Dijon, in Burgundy, in 1832. Educated at the Ecole Centrale des Arts Et Manufactures, and graduated at the age of 23. Immediately on leaving here M. Eiffel was engaged in the building of the great metallic bridge at Bordeaux and at once gave evidence of that indefatigable energy, boldness, and enterprise, which has never forsaken him and which are the marked' characteristics of the man. His remarkable capacities soon won for him golden opinions all over Europe, and he was engaged in succession on the following undertakings. At the age of 26 he was entrusted with the building of the Bridge over the Nive, in Bayonne, followed by the viaduct built on metallic piles at Comyentry in Gannat, the viaduct at Vianna in Portugal, Tardes, (near Montlucon, Cubzao, Garabit, Douro Porto, the Railway Stations of Buda Pesth, the Szegedm Bridge, &c., &c. Monsieur Eiffel's name was also prominently connected with the Paris Exhibitions of 1867 and 1878. He further constructed the Great Cupola at the Observatory at Nice, which although nearly 75 feet in diameter and weighing 100 tons a child can regulate. On the other side of the Atlantic Monsieur Eiffel's name and skill is associated with the great Statue of Liberty, which graces the Harbour of New York. It is almost needless to add that decorations and honours have been literally showered upon this great engineer."

Eiffel

Nouguier

Koechlin

Nouguier and Koechlin began working on plans for the company's tribute in May 1884, initially describing the proposed structure as "a great pylon, consisting of four lattice girders standing apart at the base and coming together at the top, joined together by metal trusses at regular intervals." For his part, Eiffel was not impressed, but he allowed Koechlin to continue working on the project and even assigned Stephen Sauvestre to help him.

After looking over Koechlin's efforts, Sauvestre decided the design needed more embellishment, so he added arches and a glass pavilion to the structure in an effort to make the building more structurally attractive. These additions won Eiffel's seal of approval, and the following year, he presented a paper on the project at the March 1885 meeting of the Société des Ingénieurs Civils, telling his audience that he believed the tower would pay tribute to "not only the art of the modern engineer, but also the century of Industry and Science in which we are living, and for which the way was prepared by the great scientific movement of the eighteenth century and by the Revolution of 1789, to which this monument will be built as an expression of France's gratitude."

Sauvestre

The first drawing of the proposed tower

When the committee in charge of the Exposition saw the plans, they were so impressed that they made Eiffel's tower the centerpiece of the event, and on January 8, 1887, the members formally contracted with Eiffel to build it on the Champ de Mars. Eiffel, acting as an individual citizen and not on behalf of his company, signed the contract and accepted the 1.5 million francs offered to defray some of the cost of building the tower, but he would have to put up the rest of the estimated 6.5 million francs in total cost himself. In return, he would receive all the income raised from the project during its first 20 years of existence.

While it is easy to romanticize the Eiffel Tower today, when it was designed, it was seen primarily as a money making venture. Near the time of its completion, one author explained,

"The natural question will arise what is to be the use of this Tower. Without entering into the scientific value to which this Tower may lead, and the many scientific uses it may hereafter be put to, we take it that first and foremost it will be one of, if not, the greatest feature of the Universal Exhibition opening on the 5th of May next. Secondly, it is undoubtedly a commercial enterprise, and we are bound to confess we see no reason why so much mud should have been thrown at M. Eiffel by part of the press, even if it turns out to have no further value. Assuredly, M. Eiffel, and those with him, have as much right to invest their money in the success of the Eiffel Tower as in any other commercial undertaking. It is calculated that about 25,000 persons can ascend per day, and taking the average cost per head to be 3fr. we have here alone a gross revenue of about 75,000 francs per day — away and apart from this there are many other minor sources of revenue, so that allowing "for all sorts of contingencies, some millions of francs may be netted by the spirited undertaker of this work, ere yet the Paris Exhibition is a thing of the past. Why call a man mad and a fool, who has sufficient pluck and ingenuity to attempt something never before attempted. We should rather blame, if blame be called for, the morbid taste of the present generation, the ever increasing craving for something new, startling and sensational. The supply follows the demand, and always will."

Few great projects ever gets completed without stirring up some controversy, and the Eiffel Tower was no exception. Since it was obvious the committee running the competition for the centerpiece of the Exposition rigged the event so that Eiffel was sure to win, there was a significant amount of hard feelings among the participants and others. Not long after work began on the project, a "Committee of Three Hundred" formed to try to stop its construction. Determined to get its opinion before the French people, the committee published the following scathing criticism in *Le Temps* in February 1887: "We, writers, painters, sculptors, architects, passionate lovers of the beauty, until now intact, of Paris, hereby protest with all our might, with all our indignation, in the name of French taste gone unrecognized, in the name of French art and history under threat, against the construction, in the very heart of our capital, of the useless and monstrous Eiffel Tower, that public spite, often marked by good sense and a spirit of justice, has already baptized the Tower of Babel. Without becoming hotheaded or chauvinistic, we have the right to loudly proclaim that Paris is a city without rival in the world. On its streets, its widened boulevards, the length of its admirable embankments, along its magnificent walks there will suddenly appear the most noble monuments ever fashioned by human genius. The soul of France, creator of masterpieces, shines from this majestic flowering of stones. Italy, Germany, Flanders, so justly proud of their artistic heritage, possess nothing comparable to ours, and in every corner of the universe Paris calls forth curiosity and admiration. Are we to let all that be debased? … To bring our arguments home, imagine for a moment a giddy, ridiculous tower dominating Paris like a gigantic black smokestack, crushing under its barbaric bulk Notre Dame, the Tour Saint-Jacques, the Louvre, the Dome of les Invalides, the Arc de Triomphe, all of our humiliated monuments will disappear in this ghastly dream. And for twenty years … we shall see stretching like a blot of ink the hateful shadow of the hateful column of bolted sheet metal."

In response, Eiffel assured the public, "I will tell you all that I think, and all that I hope. For my part, I believe that the Tower will have its own beauty. Do people think that because we are engineers, beauty plays no part in what we build, that if we aim for the solid and lasting, that we don't at the same time do our utmost to achieve elegance? Are actual conditions of strength not always compatible with the hidden conditions of harmony? The first principle of architectural aesthetics is that the essential lines of a monument should be determined by it fitting perfectly into a setting. But what condition did I need to address in the case of the tower? Resistance to wind. Well, I maintain that the curves of the four groin vaults of the monument, based on calculations, starting with the enormous and unused footing at the base, are going to taper up to the summit, will give a great impression of strength and beauty, because they will convey to the eyes the boldness of the conception in its totality. ... There is furthermore an attraction in the colossal an intrinsic charm to which the ordinary theories hardly apply. Will one argue that it is by their artistic value that the pyramids have struck the imagination of men so strongly? What are they after all, but artificial mounds? And yet, what visitor stays cold in their presence? Who has not returned from a visit to Egypt filled with irresistible admiration? And where is the source of this imagination if not in the immensity of the effort and the greatness of the result? My tower will be the tallest edifice ever erected by man. Will it not also be grandiose in its way? And why would something admirable in Egypt become hideous and ridiculous in Paris? I try to understand but confess I cannot."

A caricature depicting Eiffel's comparison of the tower to the Egyptian pyramids

    Fortunately, Eiffel had more supporters than he did enemies. A few days later, the actor Édouard Lockroy weighed in on the topic, writing, "Judging by the stately swell of the rhythms, the beauty of the metaphors, the elegance of its delicate and precise style, one can tell that…this protest is the result of collaboration of the most famous writers and poets of our time…"

Lockroy

Of course, Eiffel's ultimate vindication would be in the hands of future generations.

Chapter 2: The Employment of Iron

"In 1875, when the Philadelphia Exhibition was in course of construction, it was noted in the press that a Tower of 1,000 feet in height would be built in the middle of the park which surrounded the palace. The project, however, was not carried out, and now to France belongs the honour of having put the idea into execution. Experience gained from the erection of all high monuments hitherto constructed, has shown the great difficulty which exists in exceeding a height of 500 feet when the material used in the building is chiefly stone. Such heights as the foregoing cannot be exceeded without having recourse to the employment of iron, which is eminently suited for withstanding the oscillation resulting from the force of the wind, and which oscillation is very considerable at great heights. Metallic buildings of later construction have been easily built to a height of about 200 feet, and no serious difficulty has been felt where good engineering skill has been employed in reaching heights up to about 350 feet; but to obtain an elevation of nearly 1,000 feet, as has been done in the present instance, was a question requiring the deepest study and most careful consideration, the first being to decide definitely upon the material to based for the construction of the Tower." - *The Eiffel Tower, Paris, 1889*, published by F. C. Hagen & Co.

One of the most interesting and critical issues regarding the tower was determining the materials to be used in its construction. Traditional monuments were built of earthy, natural materials such as stone or brick, which was meant to give visitors a sense of the past, and they were often ornamented with gold or other precious materials. The Eiffel Tower, however, would be a new type of monument and thus required a new type of material: steel. While speaking before the Paris Institute of Civil Engineers, Eiffel explained the rationale: "That this material should be either iron or steel is decided—firstly, by reason of the great resistance of the metal and its light weight; secondly, by the email surface that it offers to the wind; and finally, by its elasticity, which solidifies all the various pieces and makes a structure, every part of which will bear either expansion or compression, combined with complete security. With regard to the preference that we have, for our purpose, given to iron over steel, we long hesitated, but as in our case there is no occasion that the structure should be particularly light, which, as far as the resistance to the wind goes, would be more objectionable than preferable, and seeing that steel would more readily yield to the force of the wind, and there would consequently be greater oscillation and vibration, we have chosen iron. The employment of metal for the construction further offers the exceptional advantage, that the Tower is easily removable, and if for any reason it were considered advisable to transfer it to any point away from the exhibition, this could be effected at the not very excessive cost, considering the extent of the undertaking, of 600,000 to 700,000 francs."

Of course, there were other considerations, and Eiffel detailed some of them: "We have, beyond considering metal, taken into account the advantage we should derive from using masonry, and have studied two points — one that masonry should be used in combination with the iron, and the other that masonry should be exclusively used. We will at once say that both these solutions have appeared to us, on examination, inferior beyond all comparison to the employment of metal and metal only. In endeavoring to combine the use of iron with that of masonry, one encounters all the opposite influences which would, be recognized in a mixed solution, in which altogether dissimilar elements entered. Therefore, without further remark on this point, we may add that we foresaw each difficulty in the employment of the aforesaid combination as appeared to us insuperable. We further came to the conclusion that it would be impracticable to use masonry alone, apart from the fact that the cost would be far greater."

Eiffel then went on to list his specific considerations: "The first point to be considered is what co-efficient of resistance per square centimeter or square inch to adopt. Beyond this another vital consideration has to be taken into account without which one would be entirely misled. We refer to the possible height of a Tower being only calculated on the resistance of the stone employed in its construction as if it were a monolith and one supposed that with porphyry or granite a higher Tower could be built than with good limestone. In fact, if one would not wish to make merely mathematical conceptions, and would remain in the region of facts, which one must do when studying the building of a great structure, the materials of which will be subject to a very considerable strain, it must not be forgotten that the building if of stone, could not be affected by simply placing the parts one on top of the other on surfaces more or less well prepared to receive them, as they would be inevitably separated by beds of mortar. The stability of the work would therefore depend on the mortar not cracking, and it must be, consequently, fully understood that it is the crushing point of the mortar much more than that of the stone, which must be considered, for stone by itself would appear to show building possibilities altogether deceiving, and raise practical possibilities to the most fanciful heights. The essential condition is that the material employed should be more resistant than the mortar. Classical buildings show that the cement mortar used in their construction a maximum resistance of 150 to 200 kilogrammes per square centimetre. In adopting, as a practical limit the 1-10th of this resistance, as is generally done, masonry or free-stone should not be used to support a load of more than 15 to 20 kilogrammes per square centimetre. Under altogether exceptional circumstances, and going beyond the ordinary limit of security, entering indeed to a degree the dangerous zone, as much as 25 kilogrammes is permitted. Sometimes indeed 30 kilogrammes is given as a limit, but this is altogether excessive."

In writing about the project, one author explained the science behind the structure in more detail, observing, "There is great advantage…to be gained by dispensing with the trellis bars, the weight of which becomes comparatively very great, and to give to the pile a form which would concentrate all its resisting strength in its hips, and reduce it to four great uprights, united simply by some horizontal belts very far apart. Were it merely a question of a pile to support a metallic platform, account having only to be taken, of the effect of the wind on the platform itself, which is always very considerable compared with that exercised on the pile, the wind-withstanding bars of the vertical surfaces could be dispensed with, by passing the axis at a special point situated at the summit of the pile. It is evident in this case that the horizontal force of the wind would be directly dispersed, following the axis of these rafters or stays which thus would never be subject to any great force. When, however, the building of a big pile as to be considered, such as with the Eiffel Tower, in which at the summit there is no horizontal reaction of the wind on the platform, but simply the action of the wind on the pile itself, things have to be differently arranged, and to do away with trellis bars it is sufficient to so curb the uprights that the tangents of the uprights, brought within the points situated at the same height, always meet at the point of passage of the resultant of the action that the wind exercises on that part of the pile which is below the points referred to. In fact, where account has to be taken, both of the action of the wind on the upper platform of the viaduct, and of that exercised on the pile itself, the exterior curve of the pile clearly approaches the straight line."

Chapter 3: The Noble Structure

"The building of this noble structure is now nearly an fait accompli, and, of it, it may be said that the construction of no similar edifice has ever gone on more smoothly, has been subject to fewer delays in building, nor ultimately carried to a more triumphant issue than has this magnificent monument which now stands a dignified reproach to the few who, in the early days of its conception and building, were even wont to scoff at the bare possibility of such a Tower being erected. The strongly expressed opinions of eminent scientists and others that this Tower will prove to be of positive and actual utility, both in a scientific and practical sense, will before long be put to the test ; meantime, the public will materially inclined towards the views of those who foresaw from the first that the building of the Tower would be successfully accomplished rather than give credence to the opinions of people who had denied the possibility of what has already been proved." - *The Eiffel Tower, Paris, 1889*, published by F. C. Hagen & Co.

Formal work began on the tower on January 28, 1887, and the first step was to find a suitable location for the Tower. According to a description of its progress offered at that time, "From the various borings made in the Champs de Mars, it was found that the lower stratum of the subsoil is formed by a stiff plastic clay bed about 52 feet thick, which reposes on chalk. The clay is dry, sufficiently compact, and able to bear a weight of about 251lbs. to the square inch. The clay bed is slightly on the incline from the Military School to the Seine, and is surmounted by a compact bank of sand and gravel eminently suited for bearing foundations. As far as the environs of the balustrade, which separates the Champs de Mars proper, belonging to the state, from the square belonging to the town, that is to say nearly to the height of the Eue de Crenelle, this bed of sand and gravel has an almost uniform depth of from 20 to 23 feet. Beyond this seems to be the former bed of the Seine, and the action of the water has reduced the thickness of the sand and gravel bed which gradually diminishes to almost nothing, when the present bed of the river is reached. This solid bed of sand and gravel is surmounted with a layer of fine sand of variable depth, as also with muddy sand and the like, unsuitable for receiving foundations. Certain administrative considerations forbidding the placing of the Tower on that part of the Champs de Mars which belongs to the State, and where the placing of the foundations would have presented no difficulty, the next site that appeared desirable was the quay of the Seine, so that the Tower might be as far as possible from the Exhibition buildings. The subsoil, however, in this locality proved to be utterly unsuitable, for so heavy a building could not be built directly on a clay bed, and finally, at the instance of M. Eiffel, the site was chosen at the extreme limit of the square, where the building is now situated. The foundations of each of the feet are thus separated from the clay by a layer of gravel of sufficient thickness."

Once the location was chosen, work began on the foundation that would support the structure. Due to its height and styles, there was great concern about what materials would be most suited for its underpinnings, and how those materials could best be used. The article continued, "The two rear piles, or uprights of the Tower, are situated on the borders of the old balustrade, where there was a layer of debris 23 feet deep, at which point the normal level of the Seine is reached. Below the debris lies a bed of sand and gravel, the depth of which is there about 20 feet. Thus a perfect foundation was very easily obtained for these two piles, and a layer of Beton cement, 6 ½ feet thick, constitutes the bottom of same. The two front piles have been differently founded, the sand and gravel bed here is only reached 6' 4" below the level of the Seine, and to arrive at it, marly and slimy earth, the result of the alluvial deposits of the Seine, has to be traversed. As far down as the clay, nothing could be found below the sand and gravel bed but pure sand, ferruginous sandstone, and a bank of limestone, which had formed itself at the bottom of the depression made by the water in the bed of plastic clay. There is thus an incompressible bed, which is nearly 10 feet deep at pile No. 4 (Grenelle side), and nearly 19 feet at pile No. 1 (Paris side). Thus all security is assured, particularly as the foundations are adjusted in such a manner that the maximum pressure on the foundation soil; even when taking into account the effect of the wind, does not exceed 571lbs. per square inch. Compressed air was the power employed in making the foundations of these two piles, 4-sheet iron caissons 49 feet long by 10 feet wide, being used for each pile and sunk to a depth of 16 ' 4" below water level."

A picture of the foundation

Five months later, after the foundation was completed, work began on the Tower proper. It was at this point that all the previous preparation paid off, for the architects working on the Tower had made more than 1,700 drawings of the plans and more than 3,500 detailed sketches of the 18,000+ parts that would be used. This work was critical for a number of reasons, not the least of which was the detailed mathematical calculations that played into each level. One author described the work: "Each of the four piles which form the feet of the Tower, is built in a section of 15 metres square, the pressure on the foundations being regulated and transmitted through massives or blocks of masonry, on which repose the four uprights constituting a pile. The upper part of these massives, receiving the iron shoes of the uprights, is normal to the inclination of the pile; and is of a somewhat pyramidal shape, which latter has been so arranged as to carry to a point closely neighbouring the centre of the foundation, the oblique result of pressures. This oblique reaction of pressures when it enters the masonry has a force of 565 tons without wind, and 875 tons with the wind. On the foundation soil of the two piles neighbouring the Seine, i.e., at a depth of 46 feet, the vertical pressure on the soil; is 3,320 Ions with the wind, and is spread over a surface of 90 square metres giving a load 153 lbs. per square inch. On the two piles abutting the Champs de Mars, the pressure on the ground to a depth of 29 feet is 1,970 tons, which is spread over a surface of 60 square metres, giving a load of about 471lbs. to the square inch. This surface has a covering of Beton cement. All the massives are fixed according to the horizontal projection of the uprights, that is to say at 45° in relation to the axis of the Champs de Mars. The Beton cement is composed of Boulogne cement and sand…"

For both the architects and their financial backers, the most important question concerned stability. Nothing would be worse than to get the Tower completed only to see it fall over on the first windy day. In response to any worries, the author assured readers, "In the centre of each of the massive foot, which are of Souppe's stone, are sunk two large anchorage bolts, 25 feet 9 inches long and 4 inches in diameter, which by the aid of cast iron shoes and irons, run over the greater part of the masonry of the pyramids. This anchorage, although not necessary for the stability of the Tower, which is assured by its own weight, lends, of course, additional security to it. These blocks of masonry are covered by two layers of freestone brought from Chateau Landon, which is capable of resisting a breaking or crushing strain of throe tons on the square inch, whereas the actual pressure it has to bear is but little more than 3 ½ cwt. on the square inch. The stone therefore is only required to bear one fortieth of its resisting strain. …these foundations have been made under the most secure conditions, and that be it in choice of materials, or in dimensions, they have been liberally allowed for, so as not to leave any doubt as to their stability. Notwithstanding, so as to be quite sure that the feet of the Tower can be kept, under every condition, on a perfectly horizontal plain, a cavity has been left in each of the shoes holding the uprights, in which cavity an 800 ton hydraulic press may be placed. By the aid of this press the displacement can be effected of air one of the uprights, which may be raised as required, and steel wedges inserted between the upper part of the- shoe and the lower part of a counter shoe of wrought steel on which the iron upright rests. These presses can be worked, if necessary, at any moment in the manner of a regulating screw, so as to effect the exact leveling of all points of support."

Of course, most of those visiting the Eiffel Tower would never know or much care about what lay below the surface, but the writer explaining its technical wonders understandably did, and he shared that information for those interested in it: "Around each pile, that is to say, surrounding the four massives which carry a like number of uprights and constitute a foot of the tower, runs a wall built nearly on a level with the foundations, which it encloses. For this object it is built and not for the purpose of sustaining any weight. These walls are built on pillars having arcades, the frontages of which are either perpendicular or parallel to the Champ de Mars. The enclosure thus formed is 350 feet square and is filled in with debris, except in the case of pile No. 3, under which a cellar is formed wherein the engines and generators for the lifts are stored."

A picture of the initial construction

Chapter 4: The First Stage of the Tower

"The first stage of the tower having been launched in the early part of January, 1888, the work was continued in the manner indicated, and in July of the same year, the second floor was arrived at, and this at an elevation of 377 feet from the ground. Here the four piles were joined together by means of the horizontal posts, as in the case of the first floor. At the same time the decorative arches at each of the four frontages of the tower were built, and the consoles were also put up which support the galleries that run round the first floor. For the actual erection and elevation of the parts forming the piles, nine pivot cranes, specially designed for this purpose were used." - *The Eiffel Tower, Paris, 1889*, published by F. C. Hagen & Co.

Another significant concern about the Eiffel Tower was how to keep it balanced during its construction. The engineers had designed it to be stable when completed, but during construction, it could be subject to falling if the steel rods being added were somehow out of balance. One author explained, "Seeing that the greatest inclination of each pile from its horizontal at the base of the tower is 54°, the extent to which it overhangs or is out of its perpendicular is consequently 98 feet for that part of each pile between the ground and the first floor. The difficulty of erection results from this overweighing, since it is necessary to maintain a stable equilibrium in the enormous inclined masses which constitute each foot. ...each pile is composed of four uprights, or hips, spaced in a 15 metres square, and bound together by crossbars and trellis work, thus constituting a prismatic arrangement with quadrangular base."

Fortunately, they had planned for this problem with an ingenious addition. The author continued, "Each corner upright is strengthened in its socket of masonry by the aid of a cast iron and steel support arranged in the following manner. Firstly, a piece of cast iron weighing about five tons reposes on the inclined seat of the foundation. This casting is hollow, and is bored in the side to admit of the introduction of an 800 ton hydraulic press. On the upper part of the casting rests a steel circular covering of smaller circumference weighing about two and a half tons, which partly penetrates the hollow of the under casting, at the same time supporting the lower end of the first shaft or pillar of the corner upright. The proper distribution of the weight of the upright on the masonry is assured by the interposition of the supports referred to. By the arrangement of the steel cap penetrating the cast iron support it is possible to slide the said piece of steel, which being in a sense the axis of the upright allows the definite position of each upright to be mathematically regulated, the upright being too, in a certain degree independent of the support of the foundation. It is here that the 800 ton presses…are brought into use. In the chamber reserved in the support is installed the great press cylinder the base of which rests on the iron casting, while its head works under the steel circular covering. When the press is put in operation it will lift up the steel covering and consequently raise the pillar or shaft of the upright that it supports. It is needless to say that the means of regulation, guiding, and precision are minutely calculated and by careful working a variation in the weight of the uprights can be effected to an extent that would be more than sufficient addition to the theoretical security drawn from the result of calculation, and here is a practical guarantee against any displacement in the presence of the iron holdfasts of the tower, which are anchored beneath each foundation, traversing the base of the lower iron casting being fixed by powerful iron braces to the foot of each upright."

While the hydraulic adjustments helped stabilized the structure once it was completed, they were insufficient to provide full support during its construction. That is where the scaffolding came in. One writer noted, "The great slope given to the piles, which naturally gives them a tendency to overturn. Such tendency, however, could only obtain when the pile had reached such a height that the projection from the centre of gravity fell outside the square of supports which form the base of the entire pile. Calculation showed this height in the Eiffel Tower to be about 80 feet, so that up to that point the erection of the inclined piles were effected, as far as stability goes, in a like manner to that of a vertical pile. The piles, however, having been built to the said height of 85 feet, it was necessary to find some temporary support for them until they had reached that elevation (180 feet) where the horizontal posts or rafters could be fixed, and thus join together the- four piles, forming the framework of the first floor of the tower. The method adopted in this instance was to erect wooden pylons, or scaffolds, of pyramidal shape, 100 feet in height, placing them in such a position as to support at their summit the uprights forming the piles. Twelve of the said scaffoldings had to be erected to support the various uprights of the tower, requiring nearly 2,300 cubic feet of wood. This support obtained, the building out of the perpendicular was continued to the first floor of the tower, when the first row of horizontal joists, or rafters, were fixed, thus joining the piles together. These posts are 25 feet long, and weigh 68 tons each. The great height at which they had to be fixed necessitated the erection of further scaffolding to a height of 147 feet, finishing at the top with a platform 82 feet in length. Four similar scaffolds had to be erected for each frontage of the tower, but these- together with the smaller ones were only required until the posts had been joined to the piles."

One of the most innovative features of the Eiffel Tower was its multiple elevators, designed to carry paying customers to various levels of the Tower. A contemporary brochure described how these elevators were used during construction: "Each pile of the tower, as our readers are aware, is fitted with a passenger lift, for which purpose two parallel posts to support the rolling-way or course of the cage were fixed in the foot of each pile. M. Eiffel happily conceived the idea of making use of these rolling ways for the support of a horizontal platform to receive a crane, and furnish at the same time other points of attachment for the pivot crane to work on. The cranes thus employed had a 39 feet radius, which was sufficient to serve each of the four uprights of the pile. The lifting and placing of the load was effected by the combined movements of rotation of the crane, and elevation of the platform on which the crane stood, by means of a winch worked by the crane. When the crane had thus set a floor of girders, it was hoisted, while it still had hold of its load, and until it was brought to the required height for placing the girders of another floor- This elevation of the crane was made gradually at distances of about 9 feet at a time, being aided by the application of a large screw. The crane can lift weights of four tons, and the radius could be varied 'by adjusting the jib. It was therefore capable of serving all parts coming within its reach. These cranes which were furnished with every requisite safety appliance, were powerful but easily managed machines, by the aid of which the work of erection was carried on at a great rapidity. The weight of the crane, one of each of which was supplied to each pile, was 12 tons. The pivot on which the crane worked was made to glide round a horizontal axis, so as, by means of a regulating screw to keep the crane in a vertical position. Not- withstanding the difficulty of the circumstances under which the crane had to work; it was so adapted as to be as readily and easily manipulated as if working on the ground."

The brochure later added, "The same method was adopted in lifting the pillars, girders, &c., up to the second floor. As it would have taken too long, however, to have lifted the material direct from the ground to the place where it had to be fixed, the idea was conceived of making a relay on the floor of the first stage, and for this purpose a crane worked by a six horse-power engine was there installed. The material taken from off the ground by means of this crane was raised to the height of the floor, and deposited on wagons, which by a circular route, conveniently arranged served the four piles. The metal was thus taken to the exact spot where it had to be lifted by the cranes fixed in the piles."

A December 1887 picture of construction on the first stage

A March 1888 picture of the completed first stage

A picture of construction

Chapter 5: Mathematical Considerations

"The shape of this tower has not, as is commonly thought, been designed merely in view of architectural beauty, but it has more particularly been formed on mathematical considerations, which were regulated by calculations as to the power of the wind. The tower is so formed that no matter what aerial currents are brought into contact with it, from a gentle breeze to a hurricane that beats with a force of 800 lbs. on the square foot, the result of the force which strikes each part passes by the centre of gravity of each of the sections. The form of the tower is in a manner of speaking moulded by the wind itself. One can scarcely imagine the tremendous labour that the drawing of the plans entailed. The plan of the edifice was divided into 27 squares or panels, each of which necessitated a separate diagram. Again, each of these diagrams gave rise to a series of geometrical drawings, calculated by the aid of logarithm tables." - *The Eiffel Tower, Paris, 1889*, published by F. C. Hagen & Co.

While the Eiffel Tower was always meant to be beautiful, it was also designed to be smart and was designed to the minutest detail. In fact, part of what made the actual construction of the tower move along so fast was the fact that most pieces arrived at the site pre-drilled and ready to be put into place. This was particularly important since the tower was in a precious state once it reached 85 feet in height; at that point, it was critical that the project be completed as quickly as possible. According to one pamphlet at the time, "the different metallic parts which have entered into the construction of the Tower number no less than 12,000, and each required a special drawing in which even the minutest details had been mathematically determined, notably, the size and position of the rivet holes…"The diagrams of the Eiffel Tower comprise 500 engineer's drawings, and 2,000 plans from the drawing office. Each sheet is 39 inches by 32 inches. These drawings necessitated the employment of 40 draughtsman and calculators who were engaged on the work over an uninterrupted period of two years. This staff was employed on the works of M. Eiffel's firm, at Levallois-Perret. The number of holes in the various pieces is no less than 7,000,000, and were perforated by means of a tool specially designed for the purpose. To give an idea of the amount of metal that had to be pierced, we may observe that the holes placed end to end would form a tube nearly 44 miles in length. The rivets employed in the building number 2,500,000. Each part which entered into the construction of the Tower was thus traced out, and pierced at the works situated at Levallois-Perret and on arriving at the Champs de Mars had only to be put into position and riveted on to the building."

The level of precision needed to fit together each and every pillar and rod is still amazing today. Consider the following observation: "When the junction of the four piles was being made by means of the horizontal posts situated below the second floor, a slight discrepancy was discovered in the distance apart from the pillars. This discrepancy lay in the fact that the two piles situated on the Grenelle side were rather higher than the two on the Paris side by about five or six millimetres. This slight mistake was however, rectified by lowering, and at the same time widening, the distance by some millimetres between the two pillars on the Grenelle side. This operation was effected by means of the hydraulic screw cranes."

In spite of all his careful work, Eiffel was called on again and again to reassure the public that the Eiffel Tower was indeed strong enough to withstand the winds that often whipped through Paris. On one occasion, he gave a long, technically complex explanation of the wind's impact and what he had done to protect against it: "Each of the corner ribs is supported on a square massive masonry foundation ordinarily of 6 metres in height and 8 metres square which reposes on a Beton base 4 metres in thickness and 9 metres square. These massives which are crossed by anchoring or lashers 8 metres in length, are bound to one another by a wall 1 metre in thickness and between them is a large glazed chamber, about 250 square metres which will be used as the access to the lifts and the installation of the engines. … Finally with regard to the maximum bearing strain of the iron we would observe that it should allow for a wind having a force of 300, kilogrammes per square metre which is so exceptional as not hitherto to have occurred at Paris, and we will fix this co-efficient strain at 10 kilogrammes which for all ordinary winds at Paris, will correspond to an effective strain of 6 to 7 kilogrammes. This co-efficient of 10 kilogrammes is usual in Germany and Austria for great metallic structures which are not subject as in bridges to the vibration caused by trains, we have ourselves applied it in a general manner to the station at Buda Pesth, and the Railway Companies of France also apply it to great structures."

Eiffel then concluded, "I should also refer to the extent to which a tower of this kind would bend under the influence of the wind. This question is of interest, not only as regards the actual bend which a wind of 300 to 400 kilogrammes might cause (about which no alarm need be felt, seeing that the summit of the tower would not then be accessible) but is also desirable to be taken into account so that it might be seen whether winds of ordinary violence would incommode any people who might be on the upper platform. If we take the classification of winds referred to in the work of Claudel, and calculate the bends which correspond to the indicated pressures…these figures are entirely reassuring, and as the oscillations would be extremely slow by reason of the great length of the part which was bending, it is clear that the effect would not be apparent, and would further be much less than in lighthouses of masonry, where the elasticity of the mortar is the most important factor in the oscillations that have been observed."

Obviously, just as with the questions concerning its ascetics, time has proven that the Eiffel Tower is perfectly stable and safe.

The other question raised time and again during its construction was how it would be useful to the public. As one author observed, "One of the most frequent objections urged by the public against the erection of this tower is its lack of utility." However, the same author then went on to defend the project: "We are, however, perfectly assured — and of this assurance we will presently give proof — that an actual and positive utility attaches to it, and in furtherance of this statement let us consider a few of its applications. To begin with, there is no doubt in view of the success which attended the preceding ascensions in the captive balloon, Giffard, and that of the Trocadero ascenders, that the public would find much interest in visiting the different floors of our tower, as they would thus be enabled, without sustaining either the fatigue attending the climbing of mountains, or the danger ' attached to ballooning, to view an extraordinary sight— that of a panorama of 61 to 70 miles in extent. The view of Paris by night for instance, with its brilliant lighting, would present a wonderful sight, such as is only known to aeronauts up to the present. It is not to be doubted, therefore, that this tower will constitute one of the great elements of attraction at the coming Exhibition as, indeed, after its close."

Nonetheless, the question continued to hang in the air, even as the opening day of the World's Fair drew closer: would the mere aesthetics be enough to justify the great effort and expenditure being poured into the Eiffel Tower? In the hopes of answering such speculation, the author presented the comments of Herve Mangor as to what plans were already in place for the Eiffel Tower's use: "The attention of the Meteorological Society of France has been often called to the utility of a metallic tower in open work built to a great height, from whence, by the aid of scientific instruments, experiments and operations might be made at various distances from the ground. Several observatories are fitted with towers of masonry, but for the installation thereon of meteorological instruments, more disadvantages than advantages are offered. The mural surface presented by the masonry to the heat of the sun causes eddies in the air rendering observations consequently difficult during rain, fog, dew, or snow, and thus all hygrometrical and thermometrical indications become false and illusory. The project of an iron tower 1000 feet high therefore affords the greatest interest to meteorologists."

The Eiffel Tower in May 1888

The Eiffel Tower in July 1888

The Eiffel Tower in August 1888

The Eiffel Tower in December 1888

Chapter 6: Un Fait Accompli

"The building of this noble structure is now nearly un fait accompli, and, of it, it may be said that the construction of no similar edifice has ever gone on more smoothly, has been subject to fewer delays in building, nor ultimately carried to a more triumphant issue than has this magnificent monument which now stands a dignified reproach to the few who, in the early days of its conception and building, were even wont to scoff at the bare possibility of such a Tower being erected. The strongly expressed opinions of eminent scientists and others that this Tower will prove to be of positive and actual utility, both in a scientific and practical sense, will before long be put to the test; meantime, the public will materially inclined towards the views of those who foresaw from the first that the building of the Tower would be successfully accomplished rather than give credence to the opinions of people who had denied the possibility of what has already been proved." - *The Eiffel Tower, Paris, 1889*, published by F. C. Hagen & Co.

When the Eiffel Tower was completed near the end of March 1889, the *London St. James Gazette* reported:

> "M. Eiffel awaited us with a party of fifteen, including several ladies who purposed going only as far as the second story, and my guide, who was to accompany me to the platform 275 metres above the earth where the carpenters were at work. Four or five persons who had already undertaken the ascent had armed themselves against the cold with close caps, ear-muffs and fur gloves. It seems that a tall hat offers itself as tempting prey to the furious wind and that the cold of the iron balustrades soon paralyzes the hand and sends a frightful burning sensation the whole length of the body. ... In Indian file, preceded by M. Eiffel and the guide, we entered the right pillar of the Tower leading to one of the stairways. ... The first three hundred and fifty steps, leading to a platform fifty-eight metres above the ground, are easily mounted and were constructed for the use of the public. M. Eiffel had counselled me to imitate his manner of ascent. He took each step very slowly, with his right arm resting on the hand-rail. He balanced his weight first on one hip, then on the other, giving his body a swinging motion, the impetus of which carried him to the next step with scarcely an effort. Here, however, the incline was very great, the steps gradual in proportion — so we could chat on the way, and when we reached the first platform no one was out of breath...

> "The Eiffel Tower has reached its full height of 984 ft., and the French flag was hoisted on the crowning mast yesterday. Only the lifts remain to be fitted up and the cupola at the top to be covered over. Apart from this the tower is finished. At half-past two the ceremony of hoisting the flag was performed by M. Eiffel in the presence of M. Berger, several Municipal Councilors, and a few privileged guests. This was followed by a volley of twenty-one shots. Ten or twelve persons only ascended to the little platform above the third one. All the workmen were feasted at one set of tables, and M. Tirard, M. Eiffel, and the invited guests at another. M. Eiffel made a speech expressing his satisfaction at having that day hoisted the tricolour upon the highest building in the world. Its completion was a credit to the energy and constructive skill of Frenchmen. M. Tirard also eulogized the tower and buildings, and apologized for having formerly opposed its erection, and concluded by announcing that M. Eiffel would be made an officer of the Legion of Honour. M. Chautemps announced that a commemorative medal would be awarded by the corporation to every one of the workmen, and will be distributed among them. The exhibition will open on the evening of the 6th of May with fireworks, illuminations, and a torchlight procession of 15,000 soldiers."

As was mentioned in the article, only a handful of dignitaries made it to the top of the Eiffel Tower. Among them were Nouguier, as well as the President of the City Council and several reporters, including representatives from *Le Figaro* and *Le Monde Illustré*.

Robert Henri Le Roux, under the pen name Hugues Le Roux, was one of the men in the group, and he wrote of his ascent to the top of the nearly completed Tower: "The Tower was completed…in March 1889 and, though the lifts were not yet working, government leaders and other reporters from various newspapers were invited to honor the new structure by climbing to the top via the stairs. Their trip took an hour. While the climb was grueling, the men involved found that they were able to take many breaks during their ascent as Eiffel himself paused regularly to show off some special feature."

Le Roux

A picture of the Eiffel Tower on March 15, 1889

Each new level brought a new view. Le Roux wrote, "The first aspect of this vast surface is that of a huge ship-builder's yard, in a perfect fever of work. Four great pavilions are going up at once, shutting off the view of Paris completely, at first. There are the foundations of a Flemish Brewery, a Russian Restaurant, an Anglo-American Bar and a Louis Quatorze Cabaret. They are now building wine-cellars of fifty- eight metres in extent. At the hour of repasts, this vast platform will accommodate 4,200 persons…. At one side, the windows of these restaurants open on the large empty square formed by the interior side of the four pillars of the Tower. … On the other side the diners look out on the promenade which commands the view of Paris. The aspect of the city already presented the immobility of a panorama. Life and movement had ceased. The silhouettes of people and vehicles in the streets looked like tiny spots of ink, very black, very clear, but which blotted the landscape for an instant and were gone! Those nearest the Tower had the unreal expression of the small mechanical figures which step jerkily through the little panoramas frequently exhibited in shop windows. Only the Seine seemed to live, with the waves sweeping over her muddy face, and even the river, at this distance, looked more like a bit of yellow linen laid out on the ground with the wind creeping under it."

On that frigid day, Le Roux got a view from the Eiffel Tower that few others would ever have. He explained, "We left a few of our companions here, and the rest, about ten in all, began the ascent of a small spiral staircase, rising parallel with the vertical supports of the Tower, and to which the public will not be admitted. To escape dizziness from this circular ascent we kept our eyes on the landscape, which we could see through the spaces formed by the crosses of Saint Andre, in which design the walls of the Tower are built. At almost every turn the horizon seemed to ascend with us. The Trocadero sank, apparently, until only the point of its lightning-rods touched the line of the horizon. The sombre shadows of the Bois de Boulogne, broken by one light spot, where lie the fresh lawns of Longchamp, seemed to retire into a corner of the landscape and push Paris before it toward the east."

As amazing as the view from the Eiffel Tower was, there were equally amazing things to see within the Eiffel Tower itself. Le Roux enthusiastically reported, "Suddenly the spiral staircase came to an end and we found ourselves on the second platform, at a height of 120 metres above the earth. The first objects that attracted my eyes were the wagons mounted on rails. Yes! At this height has been constructed a railroad, with its engine and cars for the furtherance of the work here, which when finished will be of less importance than that of the lower platform. It is to be a sort of bridge, or deck, with an upper deck or poop from which views can be taken, supplied with benches and settees, on which the weary may rest and regain breath and a nor mal temperature in the cool air, after the effort of the ascent. At present, nothing of all this is to be seen — there are only three rough buildings, one to shelter the machinery, an empty coach house and a canteen where meals are served for the workmen."

In spite of his amazement at the technology around him, Le Roux's attention still returned to the view he had of the fairground and the countryside surrounding it. This was the view that people would eventually come from around the world to see. "From the southern face of the Tower we obtained a wonderful view of the Exposition buildings. The glass roofs of the Machine gallery and the two palaces seemed like blue lakes of molten lead, from which rose the domes, like mountainous isles. And in the gathering darkness the mirage faded into a sombre outline and the many buildings melted into the vast nave of some gigantic Cathedral down into which we looked, from the Tower, as from the heights of its belfry. ... The four pillars of the Tower were sensibly nearer each other. The air and the light assailed me from four direct points, and with no intervening walls or buildings between me and the surrounding atmosphere I had a distressing feeling of isolation — a sensation of being suspended without the aid or support of my own limbs, in mid-air. From this height Mont Valerien had descended far below the horizon — the

Trocadero lay beneath the Bois de Boulogne — the Seine lacing them irregularly together. At my left, the hills of Meudon were almost levelled to the plain — above their shoulders I could see three swelling ranges, tinted in pale grays by the distance and the approaching twilight. At the right lay Montmartre, already in shadow — the houses with their windows minutely but distinctly marked like a tiny geometrical design. The light was nearly gone."

   By this time, Le Roux was acutely aware of just how high he was and the danger involved in being atop a not yet completed building. He admitted, "But contemplation cannot be indulged in too freely if this journey is to be finished before night fall. Again to the iron stairway! But on setting- foot on the first step we discovered that the staircase was not attached to the Tower except at the top. It oscillated sickeningly beneath us. This put a sudden damper on the zeal of many of our companions who had mounted cheerfully enough as far as the Intermediate Platform. ... We were now four. M. Eiffel, a M. Richard, the guide, and myself. We had passed the steps and were on the ladders. Here were neither platforms nor balconies — only the ladders poised on thick planks which rode the immensity of space! The ladders were lashed together by mighty ropes. Look not to the right nor to the left! Keep your eyes only on the rung of the ladder on which you are about to place your foot! After the third ladder we attained the platform 275 metres above the earth. Here the carpenters were at work. They were a dozen men, lost in space. As well as they might — abreast of the fearful wind — they worked under the shelter of canvas. M. Eiffel informed me that the wind sometimes travelled in these regions at the rate of eleven metres ten, a second — he had seen the men struggling against that, he said, and to-day it was going at the pleasant gait of five metres six, and I assure you that was enough to suffocate me ! The men worked in heavy clothing, scarfs, caps and ear muffs. As we stood there, they lifted a huge rivet, red hot from the forge, and drove it into place. The furious wind caught up the blows of their ringing iron mallets and rushed off with them, into the night. Their figures, unsteady in the gale, with uplifted arms and muffled faces were unearthly of aspect."

The completed Eiffel Tower at the end of March 1889

Chapter 7: This Stupendous Undertaking

"The Eiffel Tower! Who has not heard of this stupendous undertaking? Whatever may prove to be its merits, or otherwise, no one can deny that it is the greatest engineering work of the day, and as such it is an object of intense interest throughout the entire civilized world. Millions of visitors to the great Paris Exhibition will look upon it as one of the features of this great world's show. It is estimated that some three million visitors will be able to ascend to its dizzy height, and from its summit of nearly 1,000 feet look upon the great panorama stretched around as far as the eye will carry." - *The Eiffel Tower, Paris, 1889*, published by F. C. Hagen & Co.

When the Exposition opened on May 6, the Eiffel Tower was a huge hit. One witness wrote,

"The illuminations at night afforded a magnificent spectacle, almost baffling description. The crowd was enormous. At the signal given by the firing of a cannon all the gardens were suddenly bathed in light. ... The building of the Trocadero rivalled in point of beauty the Exhibition itself; but the supreme wonder of science was the Eiffel Tower. All its arches and main shafts were outlined with incandescent lamps. On its summit was an arc-light of immense size which utterly cast into the shade the brightness of the moon. The summit had become as a vast star, when the tower was suddenly bathed from summit to foundation in the brightest crimson light. A more extraordinary sight was, I suppose, never witnessed; and the tower shone like a beacon and could be seen at a distance of eighty miles. It was impossible to make one's way through the grounds. Extensive as they are, they were hardly large enough for the multitude which was packed in them. The main streets of the Faubourg St. Germain were densely crowded by thousands eager to see the Tower, which, as the night wore on, became the scene of more and more astonishing displays."

Almost 30,000 people visited the Eiffel Tower during the first 10 days of the fair, and what makes the number even more amazing is that they had to take more than 1,700 steps to the top since the elevators were not yet working. Once they began working, on May 26, those wanting to take the easy way to the top paid five francs for the privilege, and by the time the Exposition closed, nearly 1.9 million people had made their way through the tower.

An 1889 illustration depicting how the lifts worked

Among the most famous visitors was England's Prince of Wales (the future Edward VII) and the famous actress Sarah Bernhardt. Buffalo Bill Cody came from the United States, as did Thomas Edison. They were both at the Exposition to promote their own careers, but they still took time to visit the Eiffel Tower, and Edison wrote in the Tower's guestbook, "To M Eiffel the Engineer the brave builder of so gigantic and original specimen of modern Engineering from one who has the greatest respect and admiration for all Engineers including the Great Engineer the Bon Dieu, Thomas Edison."

Among those who visited the Tower during the Exposition were a few people with more than a passing interest in its design. Indeed, they saw the Tower not as a once in a lifetime achievement but as a possible solution to the ever increasing problem of finding cool, fresh air during the stifling summer. In June 22, 1889, the *St. James Gazette* published an intriguing article entitled

"Tower Dwellers of the Future," in which the author speculated, "For hot climates, at least, structures on the Eiffel principle would seem to offer a solution of many hygiene problems. ... The principles of construction developed in the Eiffel structure, and successfully applied on so gigantic a scale, have certainly made a deep impression on the engineering mind. ... Is the Eiffel Tower destined to remain a solitary monument of its kind, or has it opened up new possibilities for the benefit of mankind? Take the case...of the Eiffel principle being applied to structures in hot climates. The ideal of a climatic paradise would be a place which offered a ready and easy choice of temperatures, from the genial warmth of a tropical morning to the bracing cool of an Alpine slope. At night the European resident in the tropics would like to be able to betake himself to where mosquitoes cease from troubling and the languid are refreshed. ... To have some such happy mean of climate at command, it is obvious, would be an inestimable blessing—to Europeans on the Gold Coast, for instance. The practical question is, whether the resources of science and civilization are yet equal to the creation of these conditions; whether Otis lifts and Eiffel structures, with cantilever or other connections between the latter, can turn the fable of Jack and the Beanstalk into reality, and establish resorts and dwelling places at any desirable altitude. If so, then the Eiffel Tower has not been built in vain."

Illustrations depicting the Eiffel Tower and World's Fair

An aerial view of Paris during the World's Fair in 1889

Following the Eiffel Tower's triumphant run during the World's Fair, it continued to be a popular tourist attraction, with more and more people visiting it each year. When the 1900 Exposition Universelle was being planned, the decision was made to replace the lifts in the east and west legs of the tower. According to historian Robert Vogel, "When the Roux machines, the weakest element in the Eiffel Tower system, were replaced at this time, it was by other hydraulics. Built by the well-known French engineering organization of Fives-Lilles, the new machines were the ultimate in power, control, and general excellence of operation. As in the Otis system, the cars ran all the way to the second platform. The Fives-Lilles equipment reflected the advance of European elevator engineering in this short time. The machines were rope-geared and incorporated the elegant feature of self-leveling cabins which compensated for the varying track inclination. For the 1900 fair, the Otis elevator in the south pier was also removed and a wide stairway to the first platform built in its place. In 1912, 25 years after Backmann's startling proposal to use electricity for his system, the remaining Otis elevator was replaced by a small electric one. This innovation was reluctantly introduced solely for the purpose of accommodating visitors in the winter when the hydraulic systems were shut down due to freezing weather. The electric elevator had a short life, being removed in 1922 when the number of winter visitors increased far beyond its capacity. However, the two hydraulic systems were modified to operate in freezing temperatures—presumably by the simple expedient of adding an anti-freezing chemical to the water—and operation was placed on a year-round basis."

A picture of the Eiffel Tower during the 1900 Exposition Universelle

Lithographs of the Eiffel Tower during the 1900 Exposition Universelle

As was predicted, the Tower also became a source of many different types of scientific experiments. That is one of the reasons why, when its ownership passed to the City of Paris in 1909, the powers that be decided to maintain it rather than tear it down, as had originally been planned. In 1910, Father Theodor Wulf, a Jesuit priest and physicist, discovered cosmic rays while measuring the difference in the radiant energy at the top of the tower and that at the bottom.

Wulf

The previous year, according to a 1915 publication, "the Bureau des Longitudes, on behalf of the authorities interested, took the initiative in bringing about arrangements whereby the military radio-telegraphic station at the Eiffel Tower could be organized for the transmission of time signals twice daily. These signals were primarily intended to enable ships equipped with suitable wireless receivers to set their chronometers to the time of the prime meridian." The author of the article went on to explain, "It is well known how important it is to navigators, especially when approaching shore or in danger, to have the exact time of the prime meridian, the difference between this and the local time giving the longitude, i.e. their exact meridional position. Many of the shipwrecks on the coast are due to errors of position. The time signals directly supply the time of the prime meridian. If they are sufficiently exact, they also enable the rate of chronometer at sea to be determined, a knowledge of which is indispensable when out of range of the signals. Railway companies, clockmakers, etc., immediately desired to have the benefit of these signals, and at present there are a great many radiotelegraphic receiving installations intended solely for the reception of the Eiffel Tower time signals."

Following the end of World War I, there was an increased interest among aviators in pulling various daredevil stunts, and one of the most legendary was to fly an airplane "through" the Eiffel Tower. In February 1926, one such stunt cost a man his life. According to a newspaper report, "An earlier cable stated that air-man, Leon Collot, made a bet with an American that he would fly beneath the span of the Eiffel Tower. He accomplished the actual feat, but when he tried to rise the machine became entangled in an 'aerial' of the wire-less station, and dropped like a stone over the Champ de Mars and crashed through a tree to the lawn below. Flames broke out, and the pilot was burned to death, while he was in his seat in the machine and gripping the levers. Witnesses of the crash averred that the pilot made a contract with foreign cinematograph firm to fly twice under the span of the Eiffel Tower, while a parachutist was to plunge from the second platform of the tower after the aeroplane's second passage. A search was being made for the parachutist, who disappeared after the accident."

A picture of Collot flying beneath the span of the Eiffel Tower

A few years later, in 1930, the Eiffel Tower lost its status as the tallest man-made structure in the world upon the completion of the Chrysler Building in New York City, but this in no way diminished the Tower's scientific importance. On November 17, 1935, it hosted one of the earliest attempts at television transmission, and the following January, an article appeared in *Television and Short-Wave Magazine* that reported, "The new station is to work with 180 lines and 25 pictures per second. The power in the first instance is to be 1 kilowatt. The studio is in the P.T.T. broadcasting station, 103 rue de Grenelle, Paris, and it is really an old radio studio modified for television. ... Realising that at present very few people will be able to receive these transmissions the authorities are arranging to install receiving apparatus in various parts of Paris, and these viewing rooms will be open to the public. It appears that it was only in September [1935] that this latest installation was planned, and M. George Mandel, who is responsible for it, allowed two months for its completion. Actually in seven weeks everything was complete and ready for the first transmission. Considering that there was very little previous experience of high-definition work this is remarkable progress."

One of the most famous people in the world came to tour the city of Paris for the first time on June 28, 1940. Over the next three hours, he rode through the city's streets, stopping to tour L'Opéra Paris. He rode down the Champs-Élysées toward the Trocadero and the Eiffel Tower, where he had his picture taken. After passing through the Arc de Triomphe, he toured the

Pantheon and old medieval churches, though he did not manage to see the Louvre or the Palace of Justice. Heading back to the airport, he told his staff, "It was the dream of my life to be permitted to see Paris. I cannot say how happy I am to have that dream fulfilled today." That man was none other than Adolf Hitler, whose Nazi regime had just conquered France faster than just about anyone could've anticipated.

The Allies were wary of trying to liberate Paris due to its cultural significance, figuring that Hitler would order the city destroyed, and sure enough, a little more than four years after his tour, Hitler ordered the city's garrison commander, General Dietrich von Choltitz, to destroy Paris, warning him that the city "must not fall into the enemy's hand except lying in complete debris." Fortunately, that order went unheeded, and the Germans would conduct a fighting retreat through Paris in August 1944. On August 24, 1944, the French 2nd Armored Division began liberating parts of Paris, with overjoyed crowds of Parisians welcoming them, while the other Allies entered the eastern part of the city. General von Choltitz decided not to bomb Paris during a retreat, instead surrendering the city intact on August 25.

A picture of American soldiers looking at the Eiffel Tower in August 1944

Thanks to the salvation of Paris and the liberation of France, the Eiffel Tower remains a symbol of the city to this day, and it is still synonymous with all things French.

Modern pictures of the Eiffel Tower from beneath it

Online Resources

Other books about the Eiffel Tower

Other books about famous landmarks by Charles River Editors

Other books about France by Charles River Editors

Bibliography

1889: La Tour Eiffel et L'Exposition Universelle Paris: Editions de la Reunion des Musees

Nationaux, 1989.

The Engineer: The Paris Exhibition, 3 May 1889 (Vol. XLVII). London: Office for Advertisements and Publication.

Jonnes, Jill. *Eiffel's Tower* Viking, 2009.

Harvie, David I *Eiffel: The Genius Who Reinvented Himself* Stroud, Gloucestershire: Sutton, 2006.

Loyrette, Henri *Gustave Eiffel* New York: Rizzoli, 1985.

Watson, William. *Paris Universal Exposition: Civil Engineering, Public Works, and Architecture*. Washington [DC]: Government Printing Office, 1892.

Printed in Great Britain
by Amazon